WYOMING

A PHOTOGRAPHIC CELEBRATION

VOLUME 1

Published by Rick Graetz

Northern Rockies Publishing
P.O. Box 5630
Helena, Montana 59604 U.S.A.

Photographers contributing to this issue

Frank Balthis
Erwin & Peggy Bauer
Pete & Alice Bengeyfield
Francis Bergquist
Larsh Bristol
Fred & Dora Burris
Alan & Sandy Carey
David Cavagnaro
Charlie Crangle
Michael Crummett
Kent & Donna Dannen
Jeff Foott
Michael Francis
Jeff Gnass
Rick Graetz
Dan & Cindy Hartman
Christian Heeb
Dennis & Maria Henry
Jeffrey Hogan
Henry H. Holdsworth
Charles Kay
Kent Krone
Glen C. LaMasters
Jerry Long
Scott McKinley
Pat O'Hara
Barbara & Michael Pflaum
Diana Stratton
Steve Terrill
Tom Till
Jeff Vanuga
Randall A. Wagner
Nancy Wallis
Howie Wolke
George Wuerthner

2

ISBN 0-938314-78-5
Design by Linda Collins
Photographic selection and consulting by Susie Graetz
All typesetting, design and pre-press production completed in the U.S.A.
Printed in Korea by Dong-A Printing through Codra Enterprises, Torrance, California
© Rick Graetz, Northern Rockies Publishing Company 1989

Introduction

Many people think of Wyoming as the Grand Tetons and Yellowstone. While no one can doubt their attraction, Wyoming has additional magnificence in every corner of the state. The Wind River Range, the Big Horns, the Gros Ventres, the Medicine Bow Mountains, the Bear Lodge Mountains, the Red Desert, Big Horn Canyon and the Veedauwoo Rocks are but a few of the Cowboy State's areas of natural beauty.

Wyoming —A Photographic Celebration, Volume I begins an attempt to show all there is to see in the state. Let this initial volume also serve as an invitation to photographers to capture the known, the out-of-the-way places, and people at work and play in every sector of Wyoming.

More words of introduction aren't necessary. Let the images of a beautiful corner of the world tell the Wyoming story.

Rick Graetz

3

Front cover photo: *Tetons.* STEVE TERRILL
Back cover, top row left to right: *Tourist at work.* DIANA STRATTON
Cottontail rabbit. DIANA STRATTON
Downtown Buffalo. CHRISTIAN HEEB
Bottom row left to right: *Hang on cowboy!* RANDALL A. WAGNER *Sunset near Rawlins.* KENT KRONE *Wild burros near Britton Springs.* MICHAEL CRUMMETT
Title page: *After the storm.* FRED & DORA BURRIS
Facing page, above: *Snowdrift and Kit Lakes, Grand Teton National Park.* PAT O'HARA
Bottom: *Coyote posing in autumn meadow.* DENNIS & MARIA HENRY
Left: *Foxtail grass at sunrise.* JERRY LONG

Left: *Lake Marie in the Snowy Range of the Medicine Bow National Forest.* STEVE TERRILL
Above: *Looking into Wyoming from Montana, Bighorn Canyon National Recreation Area.* KENT & DONNA DANNEN
Right: *Elk calf.* DENNIS & MARIA HENRY
Following page: *Teton Range reflected in the Snake River.* TOM TILL

8

Above: *Columbines and alpine wildflowers in the Bridger Wilderness.* JEFF GNASS
Right: *Storm on Square Top, Wind River Range.* DAVID CAVAGNARO

Left: *Aspens on a slope of the Wind River Range, Bridger National Forest.* TOM TILL
Top: *State Capitol.* KENT & DONNA DANNEN
Above: *Green pastures near Dubois.* JEFF VANUGA

Left: *Popo Agie Wilderness Area, Wind River Range, Lonesome Lake.* PAT O'HARA
Above: *Grave Lake, Popo Agie Wilderness.* GEORGE WUERTHNER

Above: *The moon and the Grand Tetons.*
STEVE TERRILL
Left: *Magestic golden eagle.*
ALAN & SANDY CAREY
Right: *Sagebrush glows in the evening light at Encampment, looking across the North Platte Valley.* GEORGE WUERTHNER

Above: *Cutthroat trout with double renegade fly.* JEFF VANUGA
Right: *Marion Lake area, Grand Teton National Park.* PAT O'HARA

19

Left: *Clepsydra Geyser at sunset, Yellowstone National Park.* DIANA STRATTON
Top: *Beauty in the badlands near Dubois.* JEFF VANUGA
Above: *Emerald Pool, Black Sand Basin, Yellowstone National Park.*
BARBARA & MICHAEL PFLAUM

Left: *The Green River near LaBarge.* CHARLES KAY
Above: *Mt. Fremont, Island Lake in the Bridger Wilderness.* PAT O'HARA

Above: *Hayden Valley, Yellowstone National Park.*
GEORGE WUERTHNER
Left: *Antelope herd.* ERWIN & PEGGY BAUER
Right: *Devils Tower.* BARBARA & MICHAEL PFLAUM

Above: *Horses grazing near Bondurant along the Hoback River.*
GEORGE WUERTHNER
Left: *Indian Paintbrush, Wyoming's state flower.* FRANCIS BERGQUIST
Right: *Lichen covered rock formations at Veedauwoo Park.*
STEVE TERRILL

28

Above: *Pinyon pine tree in Castle Gardens.* JEFF VANUGA
Right: *Lake Solitude and reflections at sunset.* DIANA STRATTON

Left: *Bison herd.* JEFF FOOTT
Above: *Teton Wilderness,
the Continental Divide.*
PAT O'HARA
Right: *Badlands near
Marbleton.*
GEORGE WUERTHNER

Above: Alaska Basin Area, Targhee National Forest joining the Grand Teton National Park. PAT O'HARA
Left: Lightning near Trout Creek, Yellowstone National Park. HENRY H. HOLDSWORTH
Right: Green River and the Gros Ventre Mountains near LaBarge. CHARLES KAY

Left: *Aerial of Grand Teton National Park looking north.* PAT O'HARA
Above: *Bull moose.* DENNIS & MARIA HENRY

Left: *Firehole River, Yellowstone National Park.*
RICK GRAETZ
Above: *Cow moose with calf.* DIANA STRATTON
Right: *Erosion patterns near Big Piney.* TOM TILL

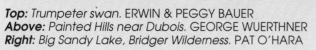

Top: *Trumpeter swan.* ERWIN & PEGGY BAUER
Above: *Painted Hills near Dubois.* GEORGE WUERTHNER
Right: *Big Sandy Lake, Bridger Wilderness.* PAT O'HARA

Above: *Red Desert.* HOWIE WOLKE
Left: *American avocet.* DENNIS & MARIA HENRY
Right: *Cirque of the Towers, Popo Agie Wilderness Area.*
PAT O'HARA

Left: *Elk in a winter morning mist.* MICHAEL FRANCIS
Above: *Wapiti Valley, Shoshone Canyon.* KENT & DONNA DANNEN

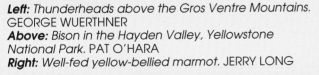

Left: *Thunderheads above the Gros Ventre Mountains.*
GEORGE WUERTHNER
Above: *Bison in the Hayden Valley, Yellowstone National Park.* PAT O'HARA
Right: *Well-fed yellow-bellied marmot.* JERRY LONG

Above: *Aspens and the Tetons near Cottonwood Creek.* DIANA STRATTON
Right: *High peaks from above Palmer Lake, Bridger Wilderness.* HOWIE WOLKE

Above: *Black bear in the autumn.*
DAN & CINDY HARTMAN
LEFT: *Crowheart Butte.*
RANDALL A. WAGNER
Right: *Red Castles, Bridger-Teton National Forest.* CHARLES KAY

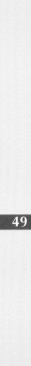

Above: *Lake Marie and Medicine Bow Mountain.* STEVE TERRILL **Left:** *Spring run-off in the Snake River Canyon.* GEORGE WUERTHNER **Right:** *Old Faithful at sunset.* FRANK BALTHIS

52

Above: *Hogback south of Lander.* GEORGE WUERTHNER
Right: *Lonesome Lake reflects Warbonnet (left), Warrior I and II (right), Popo Agie Wilderness Area.* JEFF GNASS

Left: *Monkey flowers and a pure mountain stream.* DIANA STRATTON
Top: *A prickly perch for a mountain bluebird.* SCOTT McKINLEY
Above: *Pine Hollow.* CHARLES KAY

57

Left: *Clarks Fork Canyon.* BARBARA & MICHAEL PFLAUM
Above: *Brooks Lake.* ERWIN & PEGGY BAUER

Left: *Wyoming wildlife at night.* CHRISTIAN HEEB
Above: *A brilliant carpet of moss campion.* JEFF FOOTT

Above: *Whitetail deer.* MICHAEL FRANCIS
Right: *Fall in the Tetons.* JEFF VANUGA

Above: *Castle Gardens.*
JEFF VANUGA
Left: *Flaming Gorge Reservoir.*
GEORGE WUERTHNER
Right: *Lightning Creek in the Gros Ventre.* CHARLES KAY

65

Left: Cougar drinking in a mountain pond.
ERWIN & PEGGY BAUER
Above: Arrowleaf balsamroot blooms in Sunlight Basin near Cody.
KENT & DONNA DANNEN
Right: Grand Teton and Mount Owen.
JEFF FOOTT

Left: *Winter magic in Yellowstone's Geyser Basin.* RICK GRAETZ
Above: *Working the PK Ranch, Sheridan.* LARSH BRISTOL
Following page: *Mt. Moran reflected in Jackson Lake.*
KENT & DONNA DANNEN

Left: *Aerial view of Honeycomb Buttes near Rock Springs.* TOM TILL
Above: *Mountain goat nanny and kid.* DENNIS & MARIA HENRY

Left: *Bridger Wilderness, Wind River Range.* PAT O'HARA
Above: *Moose in velvet.* MICHAEL FRANCIS

Above: *Sheepherder monument, Hart Mountain.*
FRED & DORA BURRIS
Left: *Lupine in Big Goose Park, Big Horn Mountains.*
GEORGE WUERTHNER
Right: *Autumn aspens, Square Top Mountain,*
Wind River Range. DAVID CAVAGNARO

Left: *Evening view from Island Lake in the Wind River Range. Left to right; Mt. Helen, 13,620', Sacajawea, 13,569' and Fremont Peak, 13,745'.* CHARLIE CRANGLE
Above: *White pelican rookery.* ERWIN & PEGGY BAUER

Left: *Blue Winter Creek, Gros Ventre Mountains.* GEORGE WUERTHNER
Above: *Bald eagle nesting pair.* HENRY H. HOLDSWORTH

Above: *Clark Fork Valley, Absaroka Mountains.* GEORGE WUERTHNER
Left: *Mallards in flight.* DENNIS & MARIA HENRY
Right: *Upper Titcom Basin, Bridger Wilderness.* PETE & ALICE BENGEYFIELD

Above: *Road from Cody to Yellowstone National Park.*
KENT & DONNA DANNEN
Right: *Wild Stallion in the Red Desert.* JERRY LONG

Above left: *Falls Creek in the Absaroka Mountain Range, Shoshone National Forest.*
JEFF VANUGA
Left: *Teton Range.* JEFF VANUGA
Above: *Bobcat.* ERWIN & PEGGY BAUER

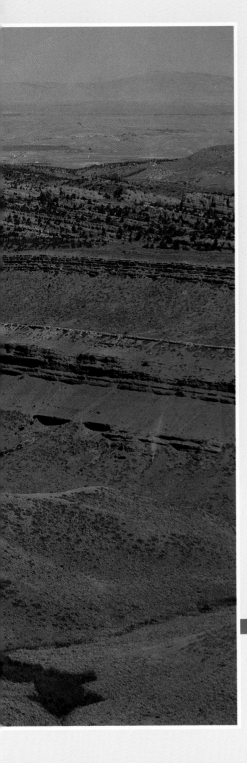

Left: *The "Red Grade"—triassic Chugwater "Red Beds"—old wagon road west of Lander.* KENT & DONNA DANNEN
Above: *Elk.* ERWIN & PEGGY BAUER

Above: *Summer wildflowers.* PETE & ALICE BENGEYFIELD
Right: *Bison calf born during a snowstorm.* HENRY H. HOLDSWORTH

Left: *Palisades Wilderness Area.* HOWIE WOLKE
Above: *Gros Ventre, Gin Pole Draw.* HOWIE WOLKE

Left: Castle Gardens.
JEFF VANUGA
Above: *Wyoming's highest mountain—Gannett Peak—13,804'.*
RANDALL A. WAGNER
Right: *Bull elk on sagebrush ridge.*
DENNIS & MARIA HENRY

93

Left: *Grand Teton at daybreak.* ERWIN & PEGGY BAUER
Above: *Mountain lion at watering hole.* ALAN & SANDY CAREY

Above: *South Fork of the Shoshone.*
FRED & DORA BURRIS
Left: *Bitterroot flowers.*
NANCY WALLIS
Right: *Grizzly bear.*
HENRY H. HOLDSWORTH.

Top: *Wind Rivers, Woodrow Wilson Peak.* BARBARA & MICHAEL PFLAUM
Above: *Absaroka Mountains.* BARBARA & MICHAEL PFLAUM
Right: *Grand Teton National Park. View from Marion Lake area.* PAT O'HARA

Left: *Mt. Everts reflected in Minerva Spring at sunset, Yellowstone National Park.*
DIANA STRATTON
Above: *Elk cow with calf.* GLEN C. LaMASTERS

103

Left: *Summer at Titcom Basin Lake, Wind River Range.* BARBARA & MICHAEL PFLAUM
Above: *Fall color in the Wapiti Valley.* RANDALL A. WAGNER

Bighorn sheep rams. JEFFREY HOGAN